# My

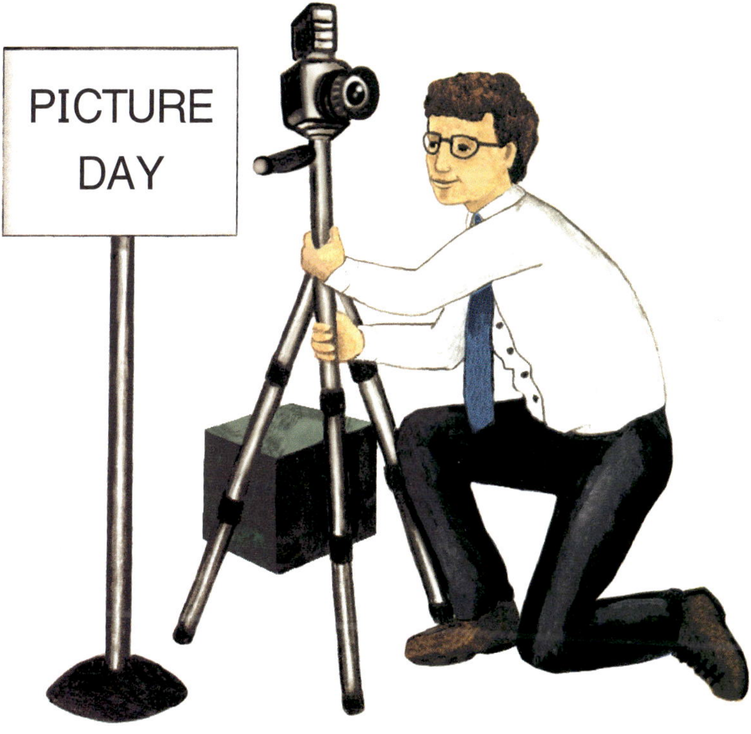


Story by Josie Stewart and Lynn Salem
Illustrations by Josh Duke

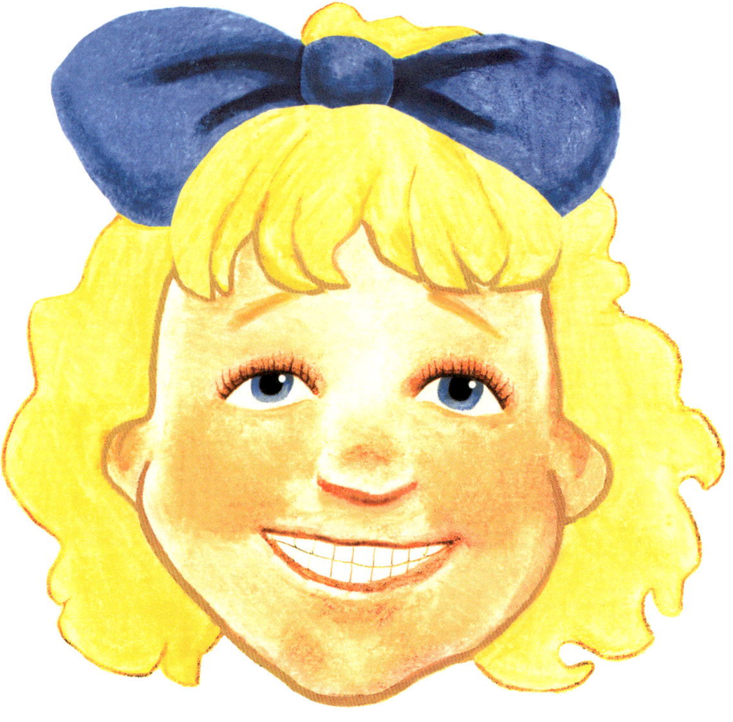

# One girl.

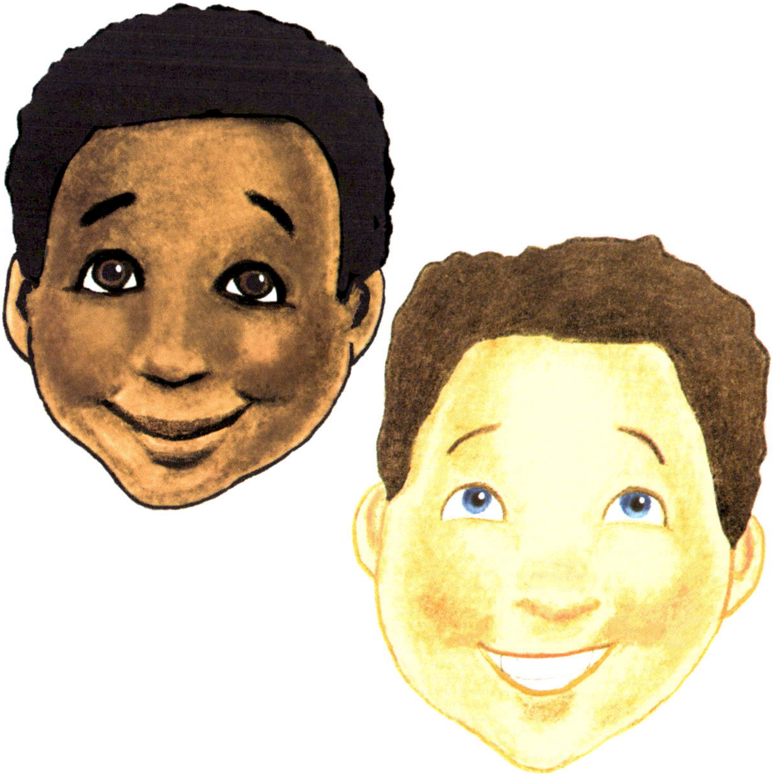

# Two boys.

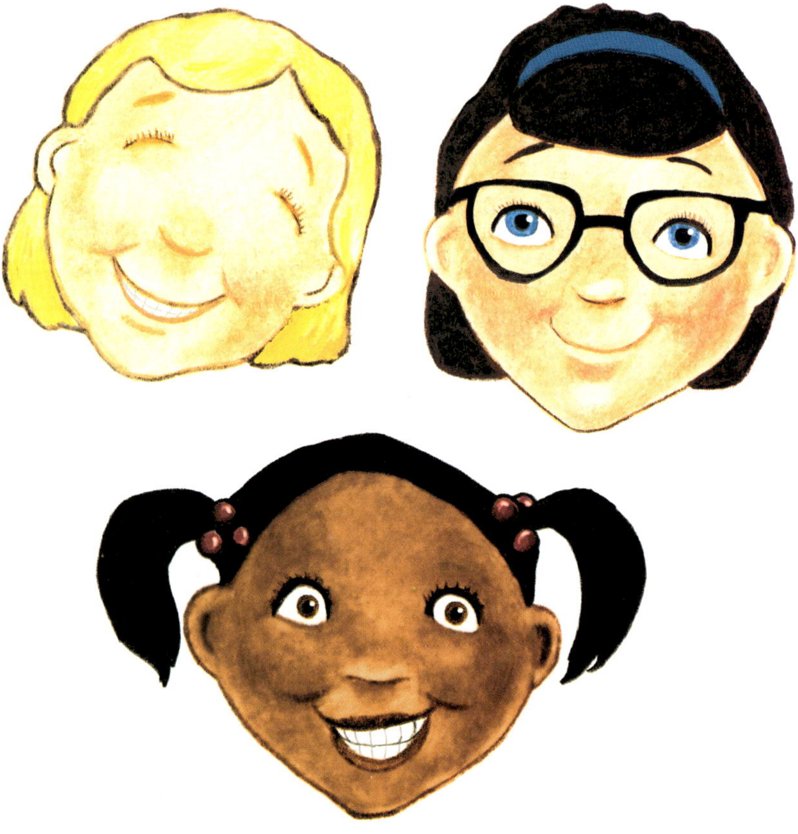

# Three girls.

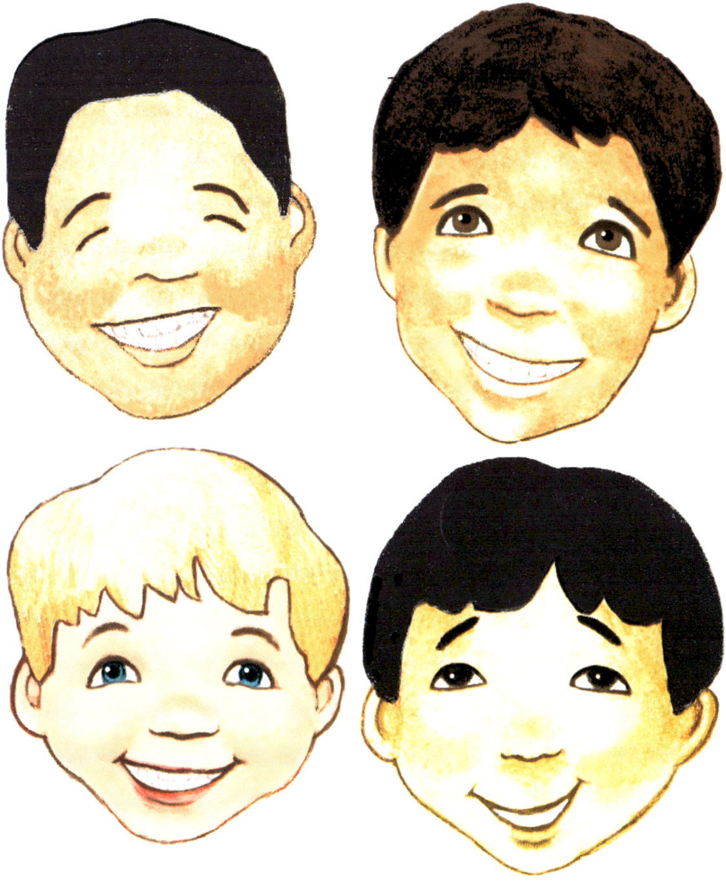

Four boys.

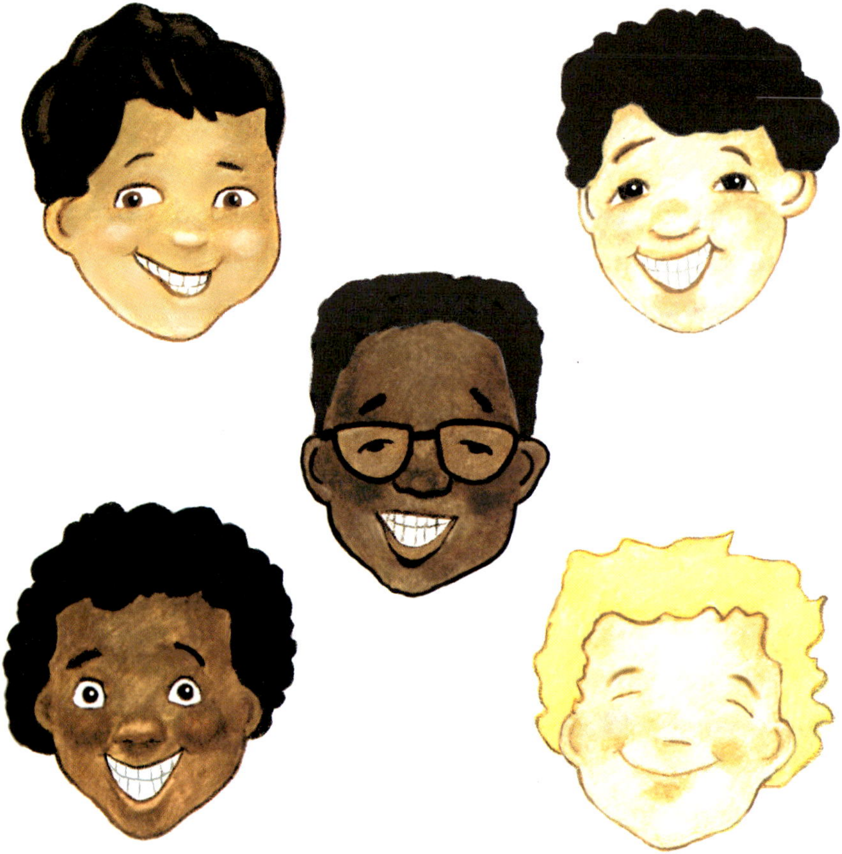

# Five boys.

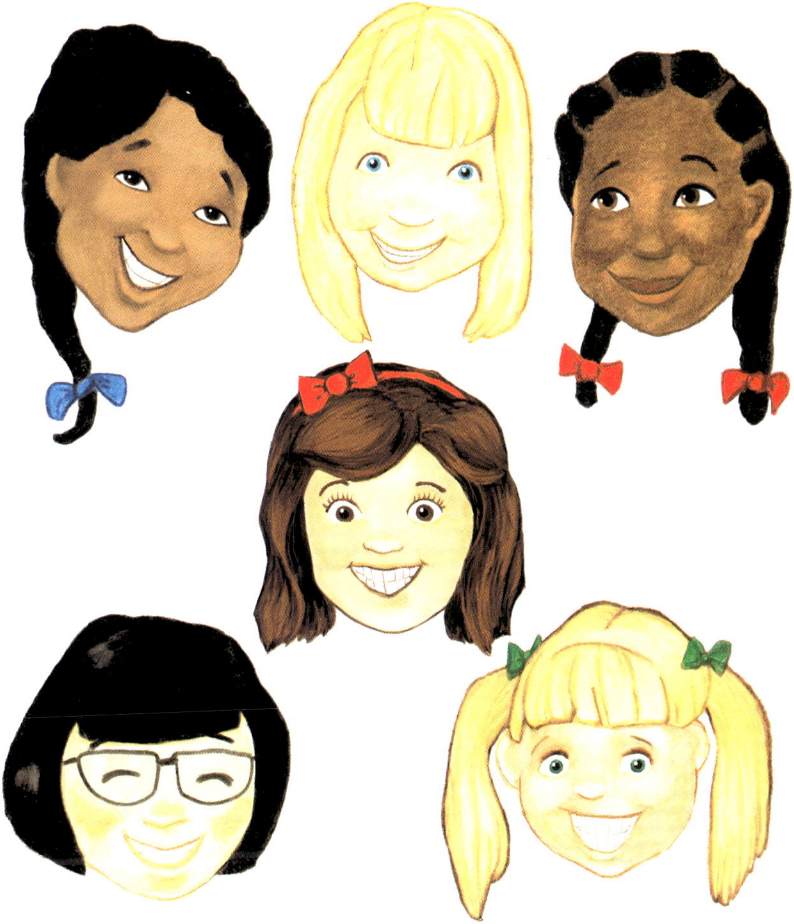

# Six girls.

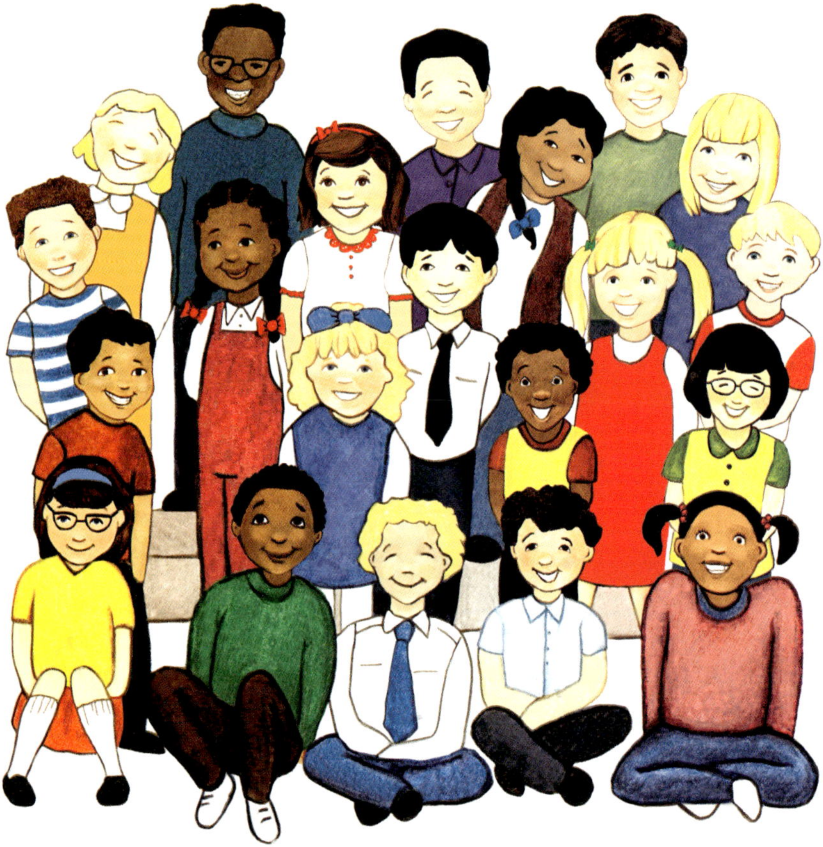

My class.